THE
WINNING FATHER

DR. T.I.M. JOOSTE

authorHOUSE®

AuthorHouse™ UK
1663 Liberty Drive
Bloomington, IN 47403 USA
www.authorhouse.co.uk
Phone: UK TFN: 0800 0148641 (Toll Free inside the UK)
*   UK Local: 02036 956322 (+44 20 3695 6322 from outside the UK)*

Published by AuthorHouse 09/11/2020

ISBN: 978-1-7283-7914-2 (sc)
ISBN: 978-1-7283-7913-5 (hc)
ISBN: 978-1-6655-8017-5 (e)

Print information available on the last page.

CONTENTS

PREFACE

The 16 days of activism to focus on the abuse of women and children in South Africa come and go every year. These days are marked by national, provincial and local marches and speeches against these horrible phenomena. Nevertheless, the abuse of women and children increases every year.

The foundation of the argument of this booklet is that the focus of these days should be changed. The focus on crimes against women and children should be on men – specifically on fathers. This should be the case because it is a well known fact that most crimes against women and children occurs in the confines of the home, where the father should be in charge.

Therefore the aim of this booklet is to start the debate on changing the way we father our children in South Africa. The premises of this booklet is that many of the men officiating in our homes as fathers (where they are absent or even present), are B-R-O-K-E-N men that needs R-E-P-A-I-Ring. (More about the R-E-P-A-I-R the B-R-O-K-EN counseling program where every letter serves as an acronym follows later on).

There are B-arriers, they experience R-ejection, they are O-ffended, K-nocked-out, E-motional drained and Negatively focused. For this reason they need repairing in their R-elationships, E-nthusiasm, Personalities, and taught to A-ccept personal responsibility with Integrity followed by the necessity to R-epent and turn to reconsider a normal, balanced God honoring lifestyle.

To attain this, the author started R-E-P-A-I-R the B-R-O-K-E-N as a counselling service to repair and retrain fathers, mothers and children in the practice of Biblical living. The dream is to train qualified R-E-PA-I-R the B-R-O-K-E-N counselors to thus start a movement to uproot the problem of crimes against women and children – by putting the focus on the fathers. Even the legal system can benefit from this initiative.

Family life in South Africa but also all around the world is in big trouble. The emergency signals are being activated on a 24-hour basis from the troubled ships in the stormy seas of family life. The home, the school, the church, the courts, the crime statistics, the everincreasing suicidal attempts, drug laundering, teenage pregnancies, school dropouts and many other factors confirm this truth: The family is in trouble and if there is going to be done something about it, it must be done very soon before it is too late. These facts addressed a longfelt need I had, to write a few notes on the crucial role of fathers in our society. In a relevant meeting earlier this year by interested parties, this need was accentuated.

I am a pastor in the full time ministry for the last 43 years, with many years of experience in counseling from my own practice. I am also a criminologist who were involved with several high-court cases where juvenile delinquency and other major offences were at stake. I was privileged to be involved in the prison ministry as a spiritual caretaker for more than 24 years.

I made a very interesting observation out of my experience in different ways working with people namely: that in every problem I ever counselled the word "family" lied at the root of every counseling problem. The family history, the family construction, family finances, spiritual state of the family, family relationships, and many other family related issues, were directly linked to the problem, crime, deviant behavior, disaster or crisis. On the success side however it was again always connected to the

"family. "

The South African Parliament and the Department of Justice is concerned to find answers for the problem of disfunctioning families in our society and the great impact it has on criminality.

The great media coverage this problem recieves in the mainline media in South Africa as well as in the whole world, challenged me. Although I am not a skilled writer, I wrote this book to highlight the plight of the broken father/s in South Africa – and what opportunities are available for them to become a "winning father."

Every year there happens to be a clear and organized effort to address crime against women and children in South Africa. There is no problem with that. In fact it is praiseworthy and should be highly recommended.

I am convinced of the fact however, that the focus must also be put on the role of men. Good men as well as bad ones. We must find out what is the good things about men and fathers in relation to family life and the education of children.

We must focus on training programs, seminars and courses to strengthen the hands of law organizations to deal effectively with the broken men and broken fathers amongst us – with the aim of healing them. We must teach the bad ones to become good ones and join the "winning father" team. We must also strengthen the good ones and motivate them even to get better.

Activism against those who abuse women and children will not heal the broken men and fathers. They need to be identified, advised, invited and trained to be winning men and winning fathers. They do not know what is right or wrong. Somebody must show them (the offenders) the way. The law must enforce offenders and make "father training courses" compulsory.

Statistics indicate that more than half of the children in South Africa daily live without their fathers or even a father figure.

We also know that most of the men who are fathers now have also grown up fatherless due to *apartheid* policies and the *trekarbeid* system of the past. Fortunately great progress took place since 1994 in the South African context. There is still a lot of work to be done.

Therefore we must also identify the problem areas when it comes to men. I believe that when men are trained to be men again as priests and kings of their households in the proper capacity God called them to be, a great positive impact can be made on the crime situation in South Africa. I am convinced that even offenders must be included when we consider the need for training of men as fathers in family issues.

It is my submission however, that women must also be included in law-enforced counseling programs. They must be trained to behave in such a way that they will not provoke their husbands. They must realise that they, together with their husbands, have an important role in the prevention of this type of crime. I prefer to call it "dark -statistics crime"

INTRODUCTION

I, together with my dear wife Joey, was privileged to raise six boys of our own. Before we started with this great responsibility, I had many theories about raising children. But after many years of leading and helping them through their secondary school education and preparing them for the challenges of adult life, I realized I needed no more theories but only grace from above.

I am also convinced of the fact that any father who wants to make a good job of his high calling regarding his family, needs the courage of Job, the wisdom of Solomon together with the grace of God to help them in their critical task of being a father (and mother).

We can either raise mastering orientated children or learned helpless ones. I still want to meet the father who wholeheartedly loves his children who does not seek the best for their future.

Every father wants to see his children happy and on the winning side of life. In order to reach this objective, he must be a winner himself. He must teach them by example. Don't do as I command you, but follow your leader and do as I do.

I confess that sometimes I was a very unwise father. Joey reminded me of my lack of wisdom and I would be quick to react with the words: "It is because of all the wisdom that the world is in such a terrible state."

Later in life as I matured in my parenting role as a father I studied the impact of a father's presence or absence in the life of his children more intensely. I became aware of the great influence of parenting styles, a father's example and the impact it has on their emotional, spiritual, physical and cognitive development. I earnestly started to pray for wisdom, I began to realize that parenting children is a direct command from God. Proverbs 22:6 states it as follows: "Teach a son in the right path and when he is old, he will not depart from it." KJV

The more wisdom I acquired in life, the more I realize that children are a gift of God and nobody can claim that we are the sole owners entrusted with the right to have children. Children are gifts of God entrusted to us to raise them up in a God glorifying way.

They are like clay to be shaped by our instructions and example, into law-abiding, society uplifting and God-fearing adults. What happens to a child (or what doesn't happen) in his family, will have a great impact on him or her as an individual, and that impact is reflected in the organizations he or she attaches him- or herself to.

This impact on a child in the family, under the guidance of the father, eventually find its way to society - and eventually on a whole nation in a positive or negative way.

Children are only borrowed to us. We saw the truth of this many times when friends of our own children suddenly died in an accident, drowned or committed suicide.

Children are blessings and not embarrassments. God needs fathers that can unlock their children's potential to the ultimate. A whole generation is waiting for the "winning father" to step forward.

We need winning fathers for if they win, there will be positive results allover. It will effect every part of our community. The crime rate will drop significantly, road accidents will decrease, deviant juvenile behavior will disappear, the economy will increase and there will be no more teen pregnancies. The list goes on and on.

<hr>

1

WINNING AS A FATHER

Fathers need to win for if they lose, the whole family, the economy, the community, and at the end the whole country suffer. Things have changed dramatically over the last few generations, when fathers mainly played the roles of provider and disciplinarian, and they were the examples of a life pleasing to God.

Fathers are given a great privilege but also a massive responsibility in the development of children. Their presence in the lives of their children leads to emotional, social, and cognitive growth.

It is further a well-known fact that the presence or absence of a father can play a crucial role in the causality of crime. Many criminals come from broken homes where the father is either physically or psychologically absent. Dr. Paul Meier highlighted the problem well. He stated that the time has come for someone to tell fathers who are not busy with that which God intends them to do as fathers that they are executing their mandates in the wrong way, and even that they are not executing their mandate at all.

It is a devastating realization that one can be a successful businessman, sports -hero, politician, manager, professor, minister of religion, or VIP, but a tragic failure as a father.

2

TYPES OF FATHERS PER DEFINITION

According to *Wikipedia,* the definition of a "dad" may include the following. (Please note that *Wikibedia* is not always authoritive but instrumental to understanding of a subject)

Biological Father

Paternal bonding between a father and a child with whom he is genetically related. This term, or just "father", refers to the genetic father of a child

Baby Daddy

This phrase refers to a biological father who bears financial responsibility for a child, but with whom the mother has little or no contact.

Birth Father

The birth father is the biological father of a child who, due to adoption or parental separation, does not raise the child or cannot take care of one.

Posthumous Father

This means the father died before the child was born, (or even conceived in the case of artificial insemination).

Putative Father

An unmarried man whose legal relationship to a child has not been established but who is alleged to be or claims that he may be the biological father of a child.

Sperm Donor

An anonymous or known male who provides his sperm to be used in artificial insemination or in vitro fertilization in order to father a child for a female. The sperm donor is also known in slang as a "baby daddy".

It is interesting to note that this type of father is only genetically involved and does not fulfill any paternal role at all. He can be known or not but most important he has no legal obligations towards the mother or child

Surprise Father

A man who does not know that there was a child until years afterward.

Teenage Father / Youthful Father

A man who fathers a child while he is a teenager.

Adoptive Father

A man who has adopted a child.

Cuckolded Father

When the child is is the product of the mother's adulterous relationship, that man is called a cuckolded father.

Please note that both parents participated in the adulterous relationship and therefore has to face the consequences together. Referring to the father whe is the only one yhat is guilty, then he can be identified as the cuckolded father.

DI Dad

This refers to the social/legal father of children produced via donor insemination (that is, when a donor's sperm was used to impregnate the DI dad's spouse).

Father-in-Law

The father of one's spouse.

Foster Father

The man who, as part of a married couple, - who raises a child though not the biological or adoptive father.

Partner Father

When the current partner of the mother of the child assumes the role of the father of her children, he is known as the partner father.

The Mother's Husband-Father

When the mother is married to a man who is not the father of her children, that man is seen by civil law (like in Quebec) as the father of the woman's children.

This type of father is also equal to being a stepfather.

Presumed Father

A man who is presumed to be a child's father whether or not he actually is the biological father.

Social Father

A man who takes de facto responsibility for a child, like caring for one who has been abandoned or orphaned. According to English law, the child is known as a "child of the family".

Stepfather

This is a married man who is not the biological father of the child. The child was born from a previous relationship. In his new marriage, he will be the stepfather to the children in this relationship.

Absent Father

A father who cannot or will not spend time with his child(ren).

Second Father

A male non-parent whose contact and support are robust enough that a near-parental bond forms. This denotation is often used for older male siblings who aid significantly in raising a child.

Stay-at-Home Dad

The male equivalent of a stay-at-home mom, where his spouse is the breadwinner.

Weekend/Holiday Father

A father who only spends time with his child(ren) on weekends or during holidays.

Sugar Daddy

A rich, older man who lavishes gifts on a young woman in return for her company or sexual favors. He has no responsibility to be a father of children. He is only interested in the woman.

— **3** —

THINGS TO REMEMBER ABOUT DADS.

My Dad

Jo-Anne Heid described her father thus:

A mender of toys	A leader of boys
A changer of fuses	A healer of bruises
A mover of couches	An attender to ouches
A hanger of screens	A councelor of teens
A poucher of nails	A teller of tales
A dryer of dishes	A fulfiller of wishes

Bless him LORD my Dad.

Who Says Men Are Not Important?

You can't spell "madam" without "Adam". You can't spell "woman" without "man".

You can't spell "female" without "male".

You can't spell "she" without "he".

"Mrs" without Mr".

And finally, we continue to say, "Amen", and not, "A woman".

According to John Wooden, "The best thing a father can do for his children is to love their mother."

Joni Ericson Tada made this powerful statement about dads: "There is nothing that moves a loving father's soul quite like his child's cry."

The following statements made by Dan Pearce when he wrote *Single Dads Laughing,* needs consideration and implementation:

Dads:

It's time to show our sons how to properly treat a woman.

It's time to show our daughters how a girl should expect to be treated.

It's time to show forgiveness and compassion.

It's time to show our children empathy.

It's time to break social norms and teach a healthier way of life! It's time to teach good gender roles and to ditch the unnecessary ones.

True sayings

In *World Peace: The Voice of a Mountain Bird*, Amit Ray wrote, "There is no teacher equal to mother and there's nothing more contagious than the dignity of a father."

Harmon Kilebrew captured the role of the father (and mother) beautifully with the following expression: "My father used to play with my brother and me in the yard. Mother would come out and say, 'You're tearing up the grass'.

'We're not raising grass', Dad would reply. 'We're raising boys.'"

Clarence Budington Kelland said about his father, "He didn't tell me how to live; he lived, and let me watch him do it."

Ruth E. Renkel put the focus somewhere else with this statement: "Sometimes the poorest man leaves his children the richest inheritance."

Be a father. Don't be "Mom's Assistant" … Be a man … Fathers have skills that they never use at home. You run a landscaping business and you can't dress and feed a four-year-old? Take it on. Spend time with your kids … It won't take away your manhood, it will give it to you. (Louis C. K.)

Two anonymous writers made some profound statements to be contemplated: "If you think education is expensive, try ignorance—especially in the field of family life where fathers must be the teachers." And, "Any man can be a father. It takes someone special to be a Dad."

The World Needs men

- who cannot be bought
- whose word is their bond
- who put character above wealth
- who posess opinions and a will
- who are larger than their vocations
- who do not hesitate to take chances
- who will not loose their individuality in a crowd
- who will be as honest in small things as in great things
- who will make no compromise with wrong
- whose ambitions are not confined to their own selfish desires
- who will not say do it "because everybody else does it
- who are true to their friends through good report and bad report
- in adversity as well as in prosperity
- who do not believe that shrewdness, cunning and hardheadedness are the best qualities for winning success
- who are not ashamed or afraid to stand for the truth when it is unpopular, who can say "no" with emphasis when the rest of the world says "yes." Harold R. Nelson

Remember as a Father:

You may perhaps try to escape your responsibilities, but you can never escape the consequences of escaping your responsibilities

Abraham Lincoln's Letter To The Teacher Of His Son

My son starts school today. It is all going to be strange and new to him for a while and I wish you would treat him gently. It is an adventure that might take him across continents. All adventures that probably include wars, tragedy and sorrow.

To live this life will require faith, love and courage.

So dear Teacher, will you please take him by his hand and teach him things he will have to know, teaching him — but gently, if you can, Teach him that for every enemy, there is a friend. He will have to know that all men are not just, that all men are not true. But teach him also that for every scoundrel there is a hero, that for every crooked politician, there is a dedicated leader.

Teach him if you can that 10 cents earned is of far more value than a dollar found. In school, teacher, it is far more honorable to fail than to cheat. Teach him to learn how to gracefully lose, and enjoy winning when he does win.

Teach him to be gentle with people, tough with tough people. Steer him away from envy if you can and teach him the secret of quiet laughter. Teach him if you can — how to laugh when he is sad, teach him there is no shame in tears. Teach him there can be glory in failure and despair in success. Teach him to scoff at cynics.

Teach him if you can the wonders of books, but also give time to ponder the extreme mystery of birds in the sky, bees in the sun and flowers on a green hill. Teach him to have faith in his own ideas, even if every one tell him they are wrong.

Try to give my son the strength not to follow the crowd when everyone else is doing it. Teach him to listen to every one, but teach him also to filter all that he hears on a screen of truth and take only the good that comes through.

Teach him to sell his talents and brains to the highest bidder but never to put a price tag on his heart and soul. Let him have the courage to be impatient, let him have the patient to be brave. Teach him to have sublime faith in himself, because then he will always have sublime faith in mankind, in God.

This is the order, teacher but see what best you can do. He is such a nice little boy and he is my son.

4

THE REAL WINNING FATHER

He Is Law-Abiding

Children learn by example. In order to train up a child in the way he or she must go, in order to end up as a law-abiding, hardworking, normal, successful, winning parent. A father must show them the good ways that leads thereto. If he is not law-abiding but criminal, he will never be a winning dad.

The good news, however, is that even the hardest criminal can change and be made new, through the power of the gospel of Jesus Christ. The Bible says in Ezekiel 36:26 that God will take out the wicked heart of stone and replace it with a good heart of flesh.

Through my many years of interactions with criminals in prison, I have personally witnessed many hopeless cases of hardcore criminals who dramatically changed, into beautiful testimony-bearers due to the power of the gospel in their lives.

I remind myself of a certain case where I was requested by prison headquarters to find jobs for three robbers. According to the officials, these men were changed so dramatically by the preaching of the gospel of Jesus Christ and repented as a result thereof, that it would be a waste of money, time, and resources to keep them in custody.

I don't really believe in rehabilitation, for rehabilitation is not permanent. It seems to lose its permanent character the moment authority is out of sight. It reminds me of the story of little Johnny, who was commanded by his mother to behave himself while she was doing some domestic errands. Needless to say that Johnny managed to keep himself in tune as long as his mother was in the vicinity. But the moment she was out of sight, he was jumping up and down on the couch again.

When she repeated the same warning thrice (that if he did not conform to the rules, he would face definite consequences), he answered her, "Mum, with my legs I will remain quiet, but in my heart, I will still jump around." Dear reader, can you see why I have a problem with rehabilitation?

I am convinced, rather, that we must start talking about regeneration. That makes real sense. Regeneration through grace makes it possible for fathers, mothers, and their children to become law-abiding citizens of our beautiful land—South Africa—driven by the law of Christ, namely love. His Spirit and His Word work in us to do His will. God's will always leads to behaviour that conforms with the laws of the country.

He Is Considerate

A real winning father has an attitude of humbleness. He considers the needs and wants of his family. He listens to good advice even from his children. He acknowledges that he is not above reproach and also needs to be ministered to.

He admits that when he is wrong and is emotional advanced enough to do it. He can use the word "sorry" and really mean it. Although "sorry" seems to be one of the most difficult words to use for all people throughout the entire world.

I remember that I ignored a yielding sign while driving one day, while my grade four son was in the passenger seat. He observed my illegal conduct and very tactfully asked me a question. Guess what was his question?: "Daddy since when do Pastors like you don't find it necessary to stop at a yielding sign?" I admitted to him that I was completely wrong and decided to leave my stupidity and stubbornness right there. I never repeated my unlawful behavior after this episode. I also confessed my violation before the Lord.

He Is Consistent

Children must never be extradited to the unpredicted moodswings of their parents. This will result in double standards because a certain decision (permission to visit a certain friend for instance) will be sometimes permitted.

At other times it will not be allowed.

A father and mother must always be consistent with their rules. Children can get confused when the rules of their parents unpredictably change and boundaries shift because of their moodswings.

Paul. D. Meier, in his book "Christian Child Rearing and Personality Development ", identifies inconsistency of parents as the main contributional factor in juvenile delinquency.

It is therefore of paramount importance that parents act in unity when it comes to discipline and rules.

They must have a united front when it comes to things that will be allowed or not. A certain TV program cannot be allowed sometimes but forbidden at another. This confuses children.

Researchers found that the great problem children have with discipline, is not by submitting to the discipline itself, but with their parent's inconsistency applying it.

The golden rule to apply when a question may arise of whose word must be followed, is to listen to the father, for he is the head and leader of his household.

This however, is not a license for him to neglect and assault his children.

Children must always be disciplined with love and not with hate and aggression. When a father assaults his child, it must not be confused as an alternative for discipline. Assault is a crime and calls for prosecution, but discipline is a deed of love which will bring many rewards, when applied (perhaps administered) in the right way.

Consistency in the behavior of the winning father reaches the target when his wife and children perceive his obedience to God. That makes it easy for them to follow and obey him.

He Is Forgiving

A father must be forgiving and by example teach his family, not to hold any grudges. Sound emotional development rests heavily on the ability to forgive those that trespass against us.

A father, in this case, the winning father, should see to it that his children learn to know the power of forgiveness when and where it is necessary.

The truth of the matter is that if we don't forgive our trespassers, they will follow us to bed, they will even accompany us on holiday.

They will reserve a special place in our daily conversations and enjoy every moment while we are in emotional pain because of them.

If the father does not forgive and teach his wife and children the same, he might become a looser. He must resolve his issues with other people in order to set the right example to his household. Bearing grudges, leads to nowhere. In facti t applies to all people, but especially to the winning father.

To teach forgiveness, the father can organize a family meeting where the advantages and disadvantages of an unforgiving attitude can be discussed. During such a meeting the father can demonstrate forgiveness by teaching them examples from his own life. Every member of the family can take a turn to do acquittal. After such acquittals, he can bless them.

I discovered the advantages of the blessing with which Jacob blessed his two grandsons, the sons of Joseph, Ephraim and Manasseh (Genesis 48:20) in my own family. When raising up children and going through life, there will be many occasions when the need will appear to forgive and forget.

Life is too short to argue and therefore the Bible teaches us in this specific example to let go of the bad, unfair, bitter, unpleasant, ugly, unwanted, sad etc. experience of yesterday (the Manasseh times of our lives) and step right into the future of blessing, gladness, joy, abundance, breakthrough, success and prosperity (the Ephraim times of our lives).

Forgive and forget. Reach for the stars. Go for gold. Don't get stuck in the desert sands of the past. Reach for your dream in the future. Bitterness and resentment brought nobody nowhere, but forgiveness provided the oil for the machinery of life to create a better and hopeful future.

We as a family did it recently and guess what? It was the best thing that could happen to me as a husband, father and grandfather. It also had wonderful results for Joey as marriage partner, grandmother and to our entire family of six boys, our daughters in law and fourteen grandchildren. What a recipe for joy and happiness. Living in the smile of God. Forgive and you shall be forgiven. And don't wait too long. The sooner, the better.

He Is Teachable

The real winning father, will have a teachable spirit. He is not a mister know-it-all. Nobody is perfect. The winning father knows that out of experience from the School of Hard Knocks (The School of Life).

Even the winning father fails sometimes but there is always the opportunity to learn some valuable lesson from somebody with experience in the school of life. He is willing to also learn from his own children.

Especially in the field of child rearing and personality develop-

ment, the winning father should be teachable. When I had no children I had many theories about child rearing. Now I have six adult boys and need wisdom from above more than ever. Wisdom comes with the years.

One of the greatest truths about wisdom is that it makes a person humble. The humble man is ready to be taught. I am yet to meet the real academic giant, who is not humble. A real educated person realizes how little he or she in reality knows about their subject. He will never be a "Johny knows it all".

The Bible reminds is that we only know "in part". This is also true of the winning father. He needs wisdom, insight and help from above.

He Is Supportive

Every person is issued at birth with the emotional needs to be loved, acknowledged and to have success.

If these needs are not met, a child will turn to negative behavior in order to find love and acknowledgement in the wrong places.

They will experiment with deviant behavior such as stealing, sex, drugs, alcohol and will even manifest enuresis at night. This is the case in order to meet their needs to draw attention on them as human beings.

Such behaviors are not well tolerated and many fathers react to that by belittling their children – not considering their own contribution to such deviant activities of his offspring. These behavior are emergency calls from our children to notice their emotional emptinesses. They are the signal torches that is fired fired from the ships in the sea of life who is in danger to be shipwrecked.

A father who is belittling or fail to love his child unconditionally and never acknowledge the child's successes, is in big trouble.

In a certain family the father and the son attended the same school approximately over a period forty years distant from each other. They co-incidently happened to have identical names and surnames. The child returned home after school one afternoon and received a proper scolding because of his "bad" report. Eventually the child asked his father if he could say something. Dad he said: "If you look closely at the report, you will see it is dated right back when you were at school. Dad,it is your own report of which you are making such a fuss about. Here is my own report which differs deliberately from the one you are scolding me for".

It is a fine art to find the right time and place to uplift a child. He should seek opportunities to motivate and compliment his child.

Parent's (especially a father's) confirmation is of great value. This is of special importance when they are surrounded by other people – family, friends or strangers – that the father should validate his children instead of belittling them.

It will be a good thing if the father can assure them of his loyalty to them in a crisis. Children need to know their fathers are there for them and that they can depend on them.

Because words can do more harm to a person than the rod, it is of great importance that a father must steer away from criticism and belittlement. The scars on the soul of a child can manifest in many ways.

There should never be a problem with a father who criticizes his child in a positive way. Positive critiscism can obtain the best results in a child. It can even serve as motivation, but he must never break a child with negative comments.

Negative criticism may even result in a tragedy. And it is so totally unnecessary. It was recently reported in the media where a matriculant committed suicide after his father criticized his schoolmarks and unfairly compared it with that of his sister. Many other heart-gripping examples can be added to this list.

He Is Calm

Aggression is not a good thing. Especially not when children are educated. A father's role is of paramount importance in this regard. Any ship has a good captain in calm waters. The winning father however will be tested time and again in troubled waters.

Some people cannot handle pressure and stress when pressure is on them. Sometimes fathers who are under stress tend to get aggressive and eventually project it to their children.

Some may swear. Others will panic. Still others will freeze or faint. Our children will observe our attitudes and conduct in the many different situations where we are provoked to aggression.

A wise father will keep his mind, his mouth and his pose in difficult situations. He knows that if he does not control his aggression, aggression may soon be controlling him.

If he reacts with a backlash of swearing, threats, negative

facial expressions and other immature behavior, he can be sure his children will be imitating it soon. Children learn by example and if they see negative behavior, they will follow it.

For this reason and many others, the winning father will be mature enough to absorb negative input and transform it into positive outcomes. I love the word of David in Psalm 141:10 (KJV) "Lord help me to pass them by".

I prefer to call it the "flicker light" verse. Sometimes on the road of life, we need to apply our flicker lights, for if we crawl behind the obstacles, it will be a waist of valuable time. Fathers who win, will steer away from aggression but control it in an adult way when it happens.

He Is Understanding

A good father will always display good sportsmanship. He has a good sense for humor. He will be able to keep a secret. He is a real sport and not a joy-breaker.

One of my grandsons who happened to be about seven years old at the time, called me aside one day and asked me: "Grandpa, can you keep a secret?"

"Yes my child" came the answer." "Will you not let me down and tell my secret to anybody else?" "No son, I promise. You can trust me completely with your most profound secret." He kept silent a few moments and came back with his final answer: "Grandpa, let's rather forget about it completely. Just forget i tand leave it as it was." Can you imagine what could happen if he told me his deepest secret and I would let him down?

One of our sons threw a stone at our neighbor's dog which could have injured him severely and I caught him red-handed.

When I scolded him about this he denied that he was guilty. I replied: "My son, either I was dreaming or walking in my sleep, but I saw you did it right before my eyes". He replied: "Yes dad, I threw the stone, but not at the dog. The dog accidently ran into the stone on the wrong moment". Now who am I not to believe him or become a spoil sport?

The Winning Father Is in Addition

- An example
- Friendly
- Morally strong
- A person of integrity
- He has a positive attitude
- He is neat
- He is hardworking
- He spends quality time with his family
- He is honest
- He is fair
- He has good humor
- He strives after wisdom
- He is a motivator
- He is approachable
- He respects his marriage partner
- He is a great forgiver
- He is reliable
- He is responsible
- He is sober
- He is hardworking
- He is humble
- He is their provider

- He is listening
- He is communicating
- He is a teacher
- He is a teammate
- He is his children's greatest secret admirer
- He is teachable
- Above all else he is always available for his children.

5

BIBLICAL PERSPECTIVES ON A FATHER

In Touch Ministries refers to the Biblical role of fathers:

When their own fathers were either absent — physically or emotionally — or poor examples, men will struggle in their roles as fathers. Do we know who He really is? The best thing any parent can do is to imitate God the Father to their children.

If we look at Jesus, God's Son, we will get a glimpse of the Father. Like Father, like Son. Jesus said, "I am the Way, and the Truth, and the Life; no one comes to the Father but through Me. He who has seen Me, has seen the Father" (John 14:6, 14:9 - KJV). Jesus is the way to discover the Father's true character.

But He is also the One who establishes a relationship with the Father for us. In Bible terms a father is the:

- Prophet
- Priest
- Nourisher
- Protector
- Upholder
- Guider
- Nurturer
- Counselor
- Commander
- Leader
- Instructor
- Guide
- Teacher
- Dissipliner
- Encourager
- Watchman
- Warner
- Godly example
- He is the life coach of his household
- He presents his wife and children to God.

The Bible gives us the real perspective of the role and responsibility of a father in Deuteronomy chapter 6. He must be a leader, teacher and informer of the ways of God to his household. He must remind, instruct and even warn them, to walk in the ways of God.

It reminds us of a little boy who asked his father who brought him

home a brand new kite. Just before he went to sleep that night, he thanked his daddy for the kite, but very seriously requested him: "Daddy, you brought me home a brand new kite, and even taught me how to fly. But Daddy, please Daddy, teach me how to pray. "

One thing that you have to notice in the Biblical view is that "father" is not in the position of a passive role. He is right in the middle of what is going on in his family. Right or wrong. What thoughts does the word "father" bring to your mind? It is so natural and forceful to think of your own father that we as sons even tend to "become like our fathers" unless we have contrary concepts set before us! However, we should look at "father" from God's perspective.

The Holy Spirit instructs, "Fathers, do not provoke your children to anger; but bring them up in the discipline and instruction of the Lord" (Eph. 6:4, ESV). The Biblical picture of father is of one who nourishes his children. He brings them up, nurtures, and rears them. He doesn't wait until something goes wrong to act. He commands, "My son, do not forget my teaching, but keep my commands in your heart" (Prov. 3:1; cf. 6:20, NIV).

He is not a cruel dictator but as the head of his household he, he is leading his household towards God. He instructs: "Listen, my sons, to a father's instruction; pay attention and gain understanding. I give you sound learning, so do not forsake my teaching." (Prov. 4:1-2; cf. 1:8, NIV).

He guides, encourages, and warns "My son, if sinners entice you, do not give in to them" (Prov. 1:10, NIV). "do not go along with them, do not set foot on their paths" (Prov. 1:15; cf. 19:27, NIV).

In his training, he is moving his children to think beyond

today. "My son, keep sound wisdom and discretion, they will be life to your soul … " (Prov. 3:21-26, NKJV).

The main focus or main part of this rendering is the direction that his nourishing takes. In all he does by word and example, he wants that child of his to be all he can be for the Lord ! That is his prayer!

In this regard, I have always appreciated David's words to Solomon as he tried to prepare him to be the kind of king God wanted him to be. "As for you, my son Solomon, know the God of your father, and serve Him with a whole heart and a willing mind." He doesn't just want him to know about God. He wants his children to be close to God! (1 Chron. 28:9, NASB). Whatever else His children accomplish, that has to come first.

When God reveals Himself to human beings, He does it by introducing Himself as a Father. To be a father according to the Bible, is a wonderful privilege but also an incredible responsibility. Fatherhood is connected in Biblical terms to:

- Accountability,
- Responsibility and
- Possibility.

The responsibility to bring up a child was not given to

- The mother only
- The day-care center
- The baby-sitter
- The school
- Grandparents or

- The Church
- But especially to the father.

If the father fails, the family is in trouble, the school is in trouble, the church fails, the society disfunctions, crime rates soar, corruption flourishes and the country cries for justice and righteousness.

Derek Prince said correctly that God left His Father imprint on every aspect of creation. "I bow my knees to the Father of our Lord Jesus Christ, from whom the whole family in heaven and earth is named" (Ephesians 3:14-15). The word "family" is "*patria*"

in Greek and derived from *pater*, which translates with father.

Therefore the best translation of this text would be "I bow my knees to the Father from whom every fatherhood in heaven and earth derives its name."

Thus in conclusion, everything goes back to the Fatherhood of God!

The winning father will be sensitive not to provoke his children according to be bitter, resentful, angry or discouraged. The reason for children's anger in many cases can be traced back to the absence of the father. The Bible commands fathers clearly not to provoke their children to anger (Colossians 3:21; Eph. 6:4, NKJV).

The Fatherly love of God reaches out to creation in all its splendor.

- The sea,
- The universe

- The constellation
- The sparrows – Matthew 6:26- our heavenly Father feeds them (KJV)
- Not one of them fall – without the Father's will Matthew 10:29 (KJV)
- Even the lions Psalm 104:21 seek their food from God. (KJV)
- Jesus came:
- To pay the price for our sins so that we may be free.

To reveal God as Father and to make us members of His family.

It is great knowing Him as:

- Savior
- Intercessor
- Mediator
- But His greatest accomplishment was to bring us back to the Father.

Knowledge of the fact He is our Father brings an end to the identity crisis many people are suffering from in recent times.

The real answer for the question "Who am I?" can only be answered satisfactorily in Bible and psychological terms for a rootless generation for those who have no sense of belonging – to get into a personal relationship with God the Father through His Son Jesus Christ. Those who know Him as their Father, has reached the end of their identity crisis.

All self-concept related problems will disappear if people

accept the truth that they are children of God. Some of our earthly fathers brought us to shame, neglected us and failed to be an example for us. Such is not the case with our Heavenly Father. 1 John 3:1 confirms: "See how great a love the Father has bestowed on us that we would be called the children of God." (KJV) Wow! Isn't it wonderful?

The good news is that although our earthly fathers may have failed us, we know that in Him we are adopted. He is our complete example as a father, He takes responsibility for us and He is our heavenly substitute. Because He is our Father we can count on it that He is never too busy for a conversation with us. He is interested in our smallest activities He desires direct relationship with us.

6

THE DIFFERENT ROLES OF A FATHER AND A MOTHER IN

Childrearing

The role of a father and that of a mother, differs radically in the child-rearing process. Louis Weiss refers to research in the 1970's which support the fact, that the roles of fathers are clearly different from those of mothers. He states the (obvious!) fact that fathers are not mothers. The way they care for, play with, talk to and discipline their children are not the same as it is the case with mothers. The role of the father is absolute in a different class, compared with that of the mother.

There is a difference in the way fathers approach their children to train them in cognitive skills and social development as well as the ways to interact in a social perspective. Their roles differ significantly.

Referring to such differences in the roles of fathers towards their children pertaining to discipline, Mare Hatwell Walker stated it well when he said: "Children respond different to fathers when it comes to discipline".

It is a fact that children respond different to a father's instructions than those of the mother. A father speaks with authority. In Bible terms, Proverbs 1:8 put it in such a wonderful way by referring to the "teaching" of a mother but the "discipline" of the father. (KJV)

According to a research report about "Fathers and Their Impact on Children's Well-Being", it was found that from birth, children who have an involved father are more likely to be emotionally secure. They adapt better to social connections and are more confident to explore their surroundings.

Fathers play in a different with their children than their mothers do. The way fathers play with their children also has an important impact on a child's emotional and social development.

The one-on-one interactions between fathers and their children with reference to stimulating and playful activity, are different from the way mothers do it. The way fathers play with their children educate them to learn how to regulate their feelings and behavior.

When a father cares and is involved in the upbringing of his children, better educational outcomes will follow. This influence and involvement of a father extends into adolescence and young adulthood. Better verbal skills, intellectual functioning, and academic achievement among adolescents are associated with an involved father.

7

"FATHER HUNGER."

I personally like the concept "Father Hunger". Our society, our families, our marriage partners and our children, crave for real fathers who are real "winning fathers". There is a need for fathers and men - real men as God intended them to be - to step forward in our society, more than ever.

A psychiatrist from Yale University, Salon Kyle, is convinced that there is a craving – a "father hunger" – present in the hearts of young people all over the world. Tandy Maglason agreed by saying that the world is bursting with boys an girls who is hungry for the presence of a loving father.

Ross-M Campbell underscores these findings by stating that "The most needy person in our society is the child and his greatest need is love". Against this backdrop, Jeremia 5:1 is a wakeup call to go into the streets of the city to find a **man**: "Run to and through the streets of Jerusalem, and see now and take notice! Seek in her broad squares if you can find a man (as Abraham sought in Sodom) one who does justice, who seeks truth, sincerity and faithfulness; and I will pardon Jerusalem – for one uncompromising righteous person". (AMPL.BIBLE)

8

FATHERS IN SOUTH AFRICA

As in many countries, having an involved father living at home can make a big difference in the life of a young child also in South Africa. For one, the household in which they grow up is likely to be better off (Desmond & Desmond, 2006; Jarret, 1994), their mother is likely to feel affirmed and assisted in her role (Richter, 2006), and their nutrition, health care and schooling is likely to be encouraged and supported (Engle, Beardshaw & Loftin,2005).

They will enjoy his protection and benefit from his position in the community (Guma & Henda, 2004).

Most of all, this- father and child – relationship will result in the receiving and giving of love.

(Lindegger, 2006).

Unfortunate, such is not the case with the majority of

South Africa's children. According to statistics, South Africa has the lowest marriage rate on the continent (Richter & Panday, 2006).

Guess which country has the second highest rate of father absence in Africa after Namibia? South Africa! (Posel & Devey, 2006).

Which country has low rates of paternal maintenance for children (Khunou, 2006) and shockingly high rates of abuse and neglect of children by men? Again it is South Africa! (Richter & Dawes, 2008).

Many of today's young fathers in the South African context, speak with sadness about the fact that they never knew their own fathers and recognize that they lack experience and guidance on father roles and responsibilities (Swartz & Bhana, 2009).

It is a sad reality that South African men commit acts of extreme violence against women and children.

This is the dark side of fatherhood in our country. Millions of children don't know their fathers and many don't enjoy the protection and care of a substitute father.

But out of this disadvantage in a country where the image of men seems to be at an all time low, arises a wonderful hope. It

appears that although the absent father is the rule rather than the exception, that father's employers after 1994, are more flexible to allow family leave and support. By way of urbanization, more fathers can be involved in their family matters. This was not the case with the "trek-arbeiders" system under apartheid. These actions result in positive involvement in family life. Although there is still a long way to go, it is a step in the right direction. There are many challenges to face and some of them are housing, job creation and education.

We can accept the fact that father's presence and involvement in the lives of children is a critical issue for social policy and programs. At the same time, the development of policies and programs need the benefit of a detailed understanding of the nature and form of fatherhood in the local context, and how this has been and continues to be shaped by historical and contemporary social forces.

9

A FATHER IS A CHILD'S GREATEST ADMIRER AND AUDIENCE.

No amount of friends can ever replace a father's presence.

When a father's right place is empty, his wrong place is engaged. No other person can influence a child as much as his father. His presence or absence is crucial when and where it is necessary.

One of our sons, were playing rugby one day. I could not be in time to attend to his game. When I arrived, it already happened to be the second half and they were behind in the score with three points. His eye caught me for a small moment and when I called his name, he got hold of the ball and scored the winning try. His father was the most important spectator in the whole place.

Nothing is more debilitating for a young person to be

engaged in a competition than to look into the stands, and find nobody cheering. When a dad is not there, the child grows up thinking my dad doesn't think I am worth something, or else he would have spent time with me".

One of the best gifts a father can give to his children, is to make quality time available for them.

I had a heart gripping experience when our oldest son happened to be in matric. I remember well one evening when he concisely approached me with the request to see my diary. He then asked me a question I will remember for the rest of my life. "Dad my I make an appointment with you?" "Yes, of course you may my son", was my reply. " But you don't need to make an appointment with me son, we are always together and we communicate on a regular base. "But Dad, that is my problem with you he said. You think we communicate. You communicate so successfully with everybody in the congregation, but when we need to communicate, you are psychologically absent. Dad hand me your diary. When is my appointment with you?"

I was disillusioned further by the shocking fact that:

- the average matric girl in South Africa on a daily basis, only has four minutes available to have a conversation with her mother
- the average matric boy in South Africa on a daily basis, only has two minutes available to have a conversation with his father

- Families don't prioritize family time anymore, eating together (at the table) where norms can be transferred and important conversations can take place
- The coming of cellphones, computers, television programs, loaded work responsibilities and other factors contributed to the failure of communication between family members. This is very crucial for fathers.

Many parents compensate for their absence, by giving their children expensive gifts. (Gifts or any material things can never compensate for their need to spent quality time as a family together).

At another occasion, our third son, wanted to show me his mathematic marks while I had a counselee in my office. I reprimanded him to consider the fact that I was busy and sent him away without making an effort to look at his good points.

When I left my office late that night, I found him sleeping on the mat in front of my office, gripping his mathematics book on his chest. Needless to say I knelt beside him, surprised to see the good marks. But we as father and son could not share that golden moment because of my ignorance and stupidity. I stood up and took the oath of Honniball that never, ever in future I would ignore a child of mine who wants to have a few moments of my time. Not even if the King of England visits me.

10

THE CRUCIAL ROLE
OF THE FATHER

Ditta M. Oliker states that there is no question about how crucial the role a father really is. A father's role is linked to:

- Educational outcome
- Teen pregnancy
- Intellectual skill
- Academic achievement
- Emotionally secure
- Verbal skills and
- Suicidal behavior

When fathered by involved, positive men, adolescent girls are most likely to form positive opinions of men, but:

Magazines, TV shows and even Domestic Courts focus far too much on the roles women play as if they are the only caregivers. They thrive on absent, alienated and divorced fathers.

Many of the reports are out of balance when manhood and fatherhood are discussed.

Many a time all the negative things men do are highlighted. For example a well-known, very popular family magazine recently sympathized with the women, fooled by their men and how they battle to forgive and forget. Shame, it is very bad and I feel very sorry for those who are involved.

But I wonder when will this specific magazine start focusing in an article on how men were cheated by their spouses. I am not incredulously, but I think it is never going to happen.And if so, it will not be in the near future. The stigma to always concentrate on the poor women with the bad men, must be changed.

It is a fact in domestic violence that women are also guilty of assault and sometimes dangerous attacks on men. In my doctoral studies related to domestic violence, it was even revealed that women were found guilty in several cases of murdering their spouses.

It is therefore worth knowing(and a fact that must not be ignored) that there can be another side to the coin. Women may be the ones who provoke men to assault them.

Women and not men only can misuse alcohol and drugs. Women can also get involved in extra-marital affairs. Men can get angry and yealous about.

If we look into the problem of crimes against women and children, we must also bring the above facts into focus. A real father and husband however, will never use violence to solve problems.

It is therefore of paramount importance and my proposal for a solution to the specific problems that South Africa has in this regard, that there is a need for training of fathers. Prevention is always better than cure.

I am personally convinced that every case of domestic violence that is reported, must not only result in prison sentences where it applies. It must also be made a command of the court that fathers (and mothers) who are guilty of misbehaviour regarding family life, must be obliged to follow a controlled training programs. If the saying applies to all other fields in our society: "If you think education is expensive, try ignorance", then it is also very true and applicable when it comes to domestic violence.

11

ROLES THE FATHER PLAY

Fathers are the backbone of the family. Girls always want a man with their father's qualities.

A man who can look after them like their father looks after their mother They will behave according to their experience. Unfortunately bad behavior will also be followed.

Anika Doggett of the Elon University in her publication:

"Juvenile Delinquency and Family Structure" discusses the following paragraphs in addition:

The least amount of communication and structure the family provides, the more likely the child will engage in delinquent activities. Findings suggest that family structure does indeed play a role in the production of juvenile delinquency. It works to both positve and negative sides of the coin.

Obviously something is going wrong in today's society.

More children than ever before in history are involved in criminal behavior.

The question to be answered is: "What provokes a child to become delinquent and what makes the child gravitate so easily towards this lifestyle?"

All ques lead to the correlation between the quality or absence of quality family life and juvenile delinquency. Research confirms that juveniles are more likely to become juvenile delinquents if there is little structure provided for them in their families.

There are several interactional influential variables, that can play a role in the comprehensive study of juvenile delinquency.

Our focus however will be on three main categories. They are:

- Family functioning,
- Impact of family disruption, and
- Two-parent versus single parent households.

A "proper" family is defined as household where two parents are in operation, there is no violence and open communication is present. Without these aspects the upbringing of a child can end up in juvenile delinquency.

It is a fact that the family is at the root of human society. Wright and Wright (1994) reported that those children who experience rejection by their parents, who are exposed to considerable conflict at home, or where supervision is a problem, are at the greatest risk of becoming delinquent.

Immarigeon (1996) states that the best way to handle juvenile

delinquency is to get their families involved in juvenile crime cases. He continues: "If anything would play a large part in delinquency it would be a family. Understanding how the family and how the juvenile within the family works, gets to the core of delinquency."

The best and most effective way to socialize a child, is through the family. It is there where children are taught to control unacceptable behavior, to delay gratification, and to respect the rights of others.

Unfortunate it is also true that the place where children learn to be aggressive, antisocial, dis-respectful and be violent, is in the family (Wright & Wright 1994). This is the place where children can be lost forever.

Positive parenting practices during the early years and later in adolescence will certainly act as buffers preventing delinquent

behavior and support those adolescents involved in such behavior to steer away from delinquency.

Adolescence is an adventurous time of expanding vulnerabilities and opportunities. It is also that time in a person's life when they get exposed to a widening spectrum of social and geographic events beyond school or family, but it starts with the family.

It is also the time of the so-called "psycho-social moratorium of values." It is during this phase of growing into a normal adult that the adolescent are involved with questions about status, salary and the qualifications of their parents. Even the name of their vehicle and brand names in clothing seems to be an important issue.

Research by Hagan & Foster (2001) indicates that if violence encompasses all emotionally environmental aspects of the juvenile's life, he or she is more likely to engage in delinquent activities.

Prochnow and De Fronzo (1997) shows that antisocial and/or aggressive behaviors may begin early. It may be as soon as at preschool level, or in the first few grades of elementary school. The tendency of the child to be resistant

to change leads to the situation where the parents start disciplining more harshly. This conduct opens the doors for continuing problems during adolescence, as well as adult criminality.

Cashwell & Vacc (1996), discuss the theory known as the coercion theory. It suggests that family environment influences an adolescent's interpersonal style, which in turn influences peer group selection.

Peers with a more coercive interpersonal style tend to become involved with each other, and this relationship is assumed to increase the likelihood of being involved in delinquent behavior. Thus, understanding the nature of relationships within the family, to include family adaptability, cohesion, and satisfaction, provides more information for understanding youth

In non-traditional families, it was found that a family's cohesiveness is a trustworthy indicator of the frequency of delinquent acts (Matherne & Thomas 2001).

The family is central in determining the future of the individual (Wright & Wright 1994).

If children are not monitored (their location, how late they will be back home, whom do they spend their time with? etc.) it contributes to delinquent behavior. This will create the opportunity to be around with deviant peers. Deviant peers on their turn are directly linked to increased deviance. (Kim, et al.

1999).

Seldom ever, there is a more crucial place where the role of communication is accentuated than within the family. Clark and Shields (1997) state that the importance of positive communication for optimal family functioning has major implications for delinquent behavior.

Communication is indeed related to the commission of delinquent behavior. Remarkable differences are shown within categories of age, sex, and family marital status.

Gorman-Smith and Tolan (1998) found that conflict and aggression between parents are early indicators of violence. Harsh parental discipline, and family conflict have also been linked).

The composition of families is one aspect of family life that is consistently associated with delinquency. Children who live in homes with only one parent or in which marital relationships have been disrupted are more likely to display a range of behavioral problems including delinquency, than children who are from two parent families (Thornberry, et al. 1999).

Amato & Sobolewski (2001) shows that exposure to parental divorce and marital discord while growing up contribute to children's psychological distress in adulthood. Social learning theory focuses on the debate that aggressive behavior is learned. Children of parents who display aggressive behavior, will learn to imitate it as an acceptable means of achieving goals (Wright & Wright 1994).

According to Juby and Farrington (2001) there are three major classes that explain the relationship between disrupted families and delinquency;

12

THEORIES

Trauma Theories

The trauma theories suggest that the loss of a parent has a damaging effect on children, most commonly because of the effect on attachment to the parent.

Life Course Theories

Life course theories focus on separation as a long drawn out process rather than a discrete event, and on the effects of multiple stressors typically associated with separation

Selection Theories

Selection theories argue that disrupted families are associated with delinquency because of pre-existing differences in family income or child rearing methods (Juby & Farrington 2001).

The third major area within juvenile delinquency and families are single parent households versus two parent households. A number of studies have been undertaken which show a very real connection between delinquent and / or criminal behavior, and single parent families.

Wright and Wright's (1994) research shows that single parent families, and in particular mother-only families, produce more delinquent children than two parent families.

Muehlenberg (2002) found indeed that the very absence of intact families opened the doors for gang membership. Children out of intact homes are more likely to get involved with gangs.

Popenoe (1997) states that fatherlessness is a major force behind many disturbing US social problems. The absence of fathers from children's lives is, one of the most important causes related to children's well-being such as increasing rates of juvenile crime, depression and eating disorders, teen suicide, and substance abuse.

The crucial role of supervision describes the reasons why two parent households are mere buffers against juvenile delinquency which is not the case with single parent homes. It all has to do with observation and surveillance. (Wright & Wright 1994).

All three of the abovementioned scenarios, seem to play a very big role in the life of the child. Family is very important in creating a law-abiding child. Separating the influence of these three main categories is a challenge.

$$13$$

THE GOOD NEWS FOR FATHERS WHO FAILED ALONG THE WAY

There is good news in spite of all the bad news of parental neglect and that is: change is possible. It is never too late to change. It is applicable to our children as well as to ourselves as fathers.

It is a fact that the best fathers fail in one or another aspect with their educational effort with their children.

We are only human beings and therefore have the possibility to fail as parents and specifically as fathers. All of us have the painfull memories of past mistakes. We feel that we could have done better.

But the main thing is that we can't change the past. If we

only succeed in making the failures stepping stones to avoid future problems, it is in order.

Therefore it will be wise to focus on the future and forget the faliures of the past.

$$14$$

STATISTICS IN GENERAL

Absence Of A Father In The UK Is Related To Misbehaving Children

- **UK Statistics**
  Sarah Hall in "Crime linked to Absent Fathers" gives the following statistics:
- A biological father having a close relationship with his children is crucial in pro-active crime prevention programs.
- She (Sarah Hall) quotes Jenny Taylor, who draws data from a study of 68 boys between 12 and 16 years of age socially deprived areas south of London. She divided them into two groups, the "good" and the "bad" boys, and compared them in risk factors for crime sexual assault, stealing and car

- theft. 55 of the good boys had fathers and 4 had no father figure.
- The role stepfathers played to decrease the risk of a boy's tendency to get involved in crime was found to be very little.

Good Boys

- 80 percent good boys had a close relationship with their biological fathers
- 55 percent lived with their fathers
- A sense of approvement and being loved kept them away from crime

Bad Boys

- 4 percent did not live with their fathers
- 45 percent had no father figure at all
- 30 percent had a stepfather
- 22 percent had a biological father not staying at home

Why Fathers Count - (Andrea Sedlack)

The social sciences study a field nowadays called "father absence" Absent fathers are linked significantly to the success or failure of children.

The National Fatherhood Initiative in the US.

Education

- Twice as likely to drop out of school.

- Children of involved fathers are most likely to receive A's.
- It was true for biological-, step- and other fathers heading single families.
- 50 percent children in two-parent families get A's while only 32,5 percent children in absent father situations get A's.

Poverty

- Where fathers are absent, children are likely to be 5 times more poor.
- According to the U.S. Census Bureau 7,8 percent of normal household children were experiencing poverty in comparison with the 38,4 percent of children in fatherless homes.
- Children with absent fathers are 54 percent more likely to be poor (Sorenson, Elaine and Chava Zibman).
- National Fatherhood Initiative confirms the above statistics.

Mortality Rates

- Infant mortality rates are 1,8 times higher for infants of unmarried women than for those who are married.
- A group of 3,400 middle school children which was studied confirmed that the possibility to develop an affective disorder quadruples where fathers are absent (Cufe, Steven P.,Robert E. McKeown).

Incarceration

Youths in absent-father households have a greater risk of incarceration when compared with those in father-mother relationships (Harper, Cynthia C. and Sarah S. McLanahan. "Father Absence And Youth Incarceration." Journal of Research on Adolescence 14 (September 2004): 369-397.

Drugs And Delinquincy

In a study of 228 students, those from single-parent homes were having higher rates for drinking, smoking, aggression and delinquency.

Sexual Activity

- Children raised by a single mother are more likely to get involved in teen pregnancy, than it would be the case when the family are complete.
- Using a pool from US and New Zealand, researchers found a strong correlation between absent fathers and sexual activity and teenage pregnancy. The risk is twice greater to get involved in sexual activity and seven times more likely to get pregnant.

Child Abuse

In a national representative sample comparing 42 countries it was found that children from single-parent families are having a greater risk to become victims of sexual and physical abuse than those who live in a normal father-mother setup.

- 77 percent greater risk to be physically abused.

- 87 percent greater risk to be harmed as a result of physical neglect.
- 165 percent risk to experience physical neglect.
- 74 percent greater risk of suffering from emotional neglect.
- 80 percent greater risk of suffering serious injury because of abuse.
- 120 percent greater risk of being endangered by some serious type of child abuse.

In disfunctionalfamilies (without fathers in charge):

Poverty   equals a 4 times greater risk regarding juvenile delinquency

Teen pregnancy 7 times greater

Obesity   2 times greater

Education   2 times more school dropouts

Mom-child-health 2 times greater risk for mortality

There is much more aggression in children where the father is absent than is the case with "normal" children.

Children born into single mothers show higher levels of aggression

Suicide Children of single parent homes are more as twice ely to commit suicide

Children with an absent father much are more likely to get involved in crime

Out of 26 offenders serving trials for armed robbery, drug trafficking and grand theft in the Broward intensive Halfway House in Pompano only one has married parents

The Florida Family Council draws a direct line between crime and missing fathers

---- **15** ----

MORE STATS

- In 2011 the poverty rate for those families without a father was 47,6 percent.
- 23,6 percent children in the US (17,4 million) lived in fatherless homes in 2014.
- A Florida study of 1.397,801 infants confirmed that the absence of fathers is linked to an increase in infant mortality and birthweights.
- A study of 263 teens between 13-18 year old adolescent woman found that girls with absent-father homes are 3,5 times more likely to get pregnant than those whose fathers are present.
- A study of 1618, Latina high school students confirmed the correlation between suicidal behavior and father absence.

- Problem behavior in children are directly linked to father's absence. Such was the case with gun carrying, drug trafficking. 279% more likely.
- Lower education and a father's role are corresponding with each other.
- A fathers role absent is connected to negative attitudes.
- Higher or lower educational achievement.
- Incarcerated fathers grew with 79 percent over the past decade.
- 55,2 percent became welfare cases.
- 37 percent public assistance cases and Section 8 housing comes from female-only households.

—————————— **16** ——————————

SOUTHERN AFRICA
STATISTICS

- In South Africa nearly two thirds of South African children grow up in fatherless homes.
- In comparisson, South Africa represents one of the highest rates of single motherhood throughout the world.
- The Human Sciences Research Council (HSRC) together with the South African Race Resolution Institute (SARRI) established in research over the
- last five years that in 60 percent cases of juvenile misbehavior, there is an absent father, in 40 percent cases the mother is single. In the US it is only 25 percent and the world average is 15 percent.

- According to research done by the SARRI, there happened to be an increase of 42 to 47 percent of fatherless homes between 1996 to 2010. This unhappy situation amongst other things seem to be contributing to a great amount of our generation's social ills and degeneration.

- More than female youth commit suicide in SA than male according to studies done by Lourens Schlebush of the University of Kwa-Zulu Natal. His research confirms there are 21 cases of suicide in SA every day. A substantial percentage belong to young people and some of the reasons are fatherless homes and domestic iolence. He also states that 7582 cases of suicide are reported every year in South Africa of which 20 times more attempts failed.

- Nigeria holds the record for stress, followed by South Africa. El-Salvador is third.

- While reliable statistics and research as to why the rate is so high are scarce, data suggests South Africans have unusually high stress levels. There is a direct link between stress and family problems.

- Viljoen also points out that mental illnesses such as depression and anxiety, comes from high stress levels and can also lead to substance abuse. In severe cases, these problems can lead to a person becoming suicidal," This is the case because of the fact that there are family fights or a poor parent/child relationship.

- The South African Medical Journal found that South Africa already has high rates of substance abuse with, for example, alcohol alone being the thirdhighest contributor to death and disability among citizens, according to a 2014 study published in the South African Medical Journal.

$$17$$

THE MILLION DOLLAR, NO RATHER A BILLION DOLLAR QUESTION

It is very clear out of what has been said, that the high cost of neglect in relation to the vital role men and fathers play, cannot be ignored any longer.

In South Africa the judicial system gives great prominence to crimes against women and children. But somewhere the need to acknowledge the positive roles men can play as well as the destructive ones in the absence of the conforming behavior, disappear.

The father's crucial role in emotional development education, financial matters and discipline, seems to be only prominent when the law system considers sentences on behalf of women when grants are assigned.

Can Any Country Afford this any longer?

I want to ask a million dollar question, no rather a billion dollar one. Can any society or budget of any country in the world, more specific, the South African budget, afford the luxury to avoid the father factor in our midst?

If the answer is no, then it is time for a national wake-up call. Every father should stand up and decide to make a difference. This decision fathers make, must not only be the result from external forces but also from deep within.

We as a country can't afford to see another child drawn away into drug addiction. We can't afford to see one more beautiful teenager to commit suicide.

We can't afford to see one more family breakup. It is time to stand up and speak up as fathers. We can't afford the luxury of negligence one day longer. The material we are working with is too precious to waste.

We can't afford to see another battered face in the front pages of the media anymore. We can't afford to hear of another murder or cruel crime that was committed against guiltless children or their mothers. It is time to take action. It is time for the real men to stand up.

War is declared by our president Cyril Ramaphosa, our government and many other organisations and individuals on the crime of violence against women and children. It is a really praiseworthy thing.

The great need of the hour however in domestic violence and crimes against women and children in South Africa, is traing for the accused and not cheap rehtorical speech.

Real training for men that will result in heart-changing and revolutionary life changing. And it is possible.

My experience comes from over more than thrity years in the counceliing practice as well as in the full-time minsitry. It is my submission that there are too many cases that have been withdrawn and criminals even after sentencing, escapes with unwanted behavior in many different ways.

Enforce counseling by making it a court order

The court gives them an option to enroll on counselling courses out of free will. This option must be replaced by a court order. They must be forced by law to participate in an effective "father training programme." A programme where they can meet themselves in the mirror of live.

Prevention is always better than cure. Even the employers and the whole businessworld can listen. What is more important. Greater profits or better families. This will lead to working hours that may be adjusted in order to accomodate the needs of families in South Africa.

All of us know the labour market has many challenges. To be employed in South Africa as well as the rest of the world, is a great privilege. Employers in order to survive, requires a maximum effort from their employees. This is generally reflected in working hours.

But I am convinced of the fact that somewhere a solution can be found where businesses will realise that the greatest assett of their businesses is not money, property or something else. The most valuable asset of any organisation lies in its personel. Society in taking hands with the labour market through good planning, can help to create a family-focused environment by making it possible to meet the needs of a "father hunger" world.

Nearer home

The time for a radical spiritual check-up has arrived. What about family devotions? What about organising an evening with the aim to bless your family? What about going to church

together as a family and fill your right place on a Sunday morning instead of making hundred excuses why you can't go? What about reconsidering right priorities and make a clear decision between living standard and living quality.

The time has come for every father who wants to become a winning father to take a firm stand and build his house on the rock.

What about starting to build strong family ties by turning back to the good old days of spending quality time together at the table.

Hasn't the time arrived to switch of the TV and start communicating as a family again? Especialy those in the role of fatehers? Isn't it time os tart living again instead of surviving only?

It all starts with us as fathers.We can make a difference. Build your house on the Rock and it shall stand. Don't compromise for the second best. God needs men. Good men. Strong men. Wise men. Men that know that they know that they know He is in control.

Remember the words of Justus Tsungu once addressing a group of criminologists at UNISA : "We can feed the hungry, we can educate the unlearned and we can finance the needy, but if we fail to give them a proper knowledge of the Bible, we will leave their hearts empty. And who is going to fill this emptiness? Alcoholism, secularism, satanism and ALL other isms will do it."

18

SUGGESTIONS

I really feel strong about it that there must come a definite, organised effort to address fatherhood, family life, role models etc. Positive fatherhood are learned behavior. Things can and must be changed.

Considering all that was said above I want to suggest today that the following will get priority attention:

1. Formal family education and training programs must be developed by people with the right credentials to setup a national training strategy for

- Domestic Court Officials
- Corrective Service
- The Police Force
- Churches
- Curricula in Universities, Colleges and Schools
- Sport clubs

- Marriage officers and
- Schools

This training must be an ongoing exercise (for example a 10 year plan) and not a once-off effort.

2. That the offenders in domestic violence cases will be enforced by law (part of their sentences) to take part in Family
3. training programs.
4. Education in family life with special focus on the role of a father.
5. Teeth will be given to counselors to make rehabilitation programs compulsory. It must not be a matter of choice but rather ordered by court.
6. Laws must be passed that will strengthen the hands of counselors to make it compulsory for offenders to participate in rehabilitation programs or family guidance clinics.
7. It must not be possible for a women to withdraw a domestic violence or assault case. Every such case must follow the legal procedure but offenders must be forced by law, to follow a rehabilitation course for example R-E-P-A-I-R- the B-R-O-K-E-N-.

In South Africa the judicial system gives great prominence to crimes against women and children. But somewhere along the lines, the need to acknowledge the positive roles men can play as well as the destructive ones in the absence of the conforming behavior, disappear or are just summarily ignored.

I may be completely wrong but the impression I get is not encouraging. The father's crucial role in emotional development education, financial matters, and discipline, seems to be only prominent when the law system considers sentences on behalf of women when grants are assigned.

There are hundreds of organizations to promote the rights of women and children before the law, especially with regard to crime and domestic violence. I have no problem with that at all. When women and children become the victims of crime, the culprits must meet with the full force of the law.

What challenges me farther is a few questions:

- Where are the organizations for men?
- Is there any of the abovementioned organizations functioning in our society and if they are there, why don't we hear from them?
- What happens to the offenders found guilty? Do we put them in custody and release them after a specific timeline connected to their offence, but fail to address their crimes in order to break the unhappy and unhealthy cycle in our society? We must start acting and provide pro-active strategies.

An American Example:

Up to $50 million per year may be awarded to government entities, faith-based organizations or community organizations to fund activities promoting responsible fatherhood. Such activities may include parent education, counseling, education and career services to foster fathers' economic stability, or a national media campaign to encourage appropriate parent involvement in a child's life.

Up to $2 million per year may be awarded as competitive grants to Indian tribes to demonstrate the effectiveness of coordinating the provision of child welfare and TANF services to tribal families at risk of child abuse or neglect.

The remaining funds are designated for healthy marriage activities, which may include programs of premarital education, conflict resolution, marriage enhancement for married couples and programs designed to reduce disincentives to marriage in means-tested aid."

Isn't this a worthy example to follow? Some critics may say all this won't help? I say: How will we know if we don't try?

I strongly believe by doing this, a great impact will be made in the right direction.

Let us never get weary in our efforts to develop a buffer against the destructive forces of darkness that targets the family. There is hope. There is a future. But the time to start working is today.

Remember: If we plan for one year we plant maize. If we plan for ten years, we plant trees. But if we plan for the future we educate young people.

If you think education is expensive, try ignorance. Let us use the opportunity to train winning fathers. It will turn out to be one of the best investments ever.

T.I.M. Jooste

SOURCES

Anderson K. Relatedness and investment in children in South Africa. Human Nature. 2005;16:1–31

Anderson, Amy L. " Individual and contextual influences on delinquency: the role of the single parent family." Journal of Criminal Justice 30 (November 2002): 575-587.

Baba: Men and fatherhood in South Africa. HSRC Press; Cape Town: 2006. pp. 306–316.

Beardshaw T. Taking forward work with men in families. In: Richter L, Morrell R, editors.

Bonthuys E. Realizing South African children's basic socio-economic claims against parents and the state: What courts can achieve. International Journal of Law, Policy and the Family. 2008;22:333–355.

Caribbean Child Development Centre, S. o. C. S. Men and their families: Discussion guide for use by groups in church, school, community and other settings. University of the West Indies; Kingston, Jamaica: 1994.

Case A, Hosegood V, Lund F. The reach and impact of Child Support

Grants: Evidence from KwaZulu-Natal. Development Southern Africa. 2005;22:467–482.

Chikovore J, Nyström L, Lindmark G, Ahlberg B. Denial and violence: Paradoxes in male perspectives to premarital sex and pregnancy in rural Zimbabwe. African Sociological Review. 2003;7:53–72.

Child, Youth, Family and Social Development (CYFSD). Human Sciences Research Council. Intuthuko Junction.

Department of Social Development . National Family Policy (June), final draft. Department of Social Development; Pretoria: 2006.

Focus on the employment standards Bill: Defend Worker Rights! COSATU; 1996.

Cuffe, Steven P.,Robert E. McKeown, Cherryl L. Addy, and Carol Z.

Garrison. "Family Psychosocial Risk Factors in a Longitudinal Epidemiological Study of Adolescents." Journal of American Academic Child Adolescent Psychiatry 44 (February 2005): 121-129.

Ellis, Bruce J., John E Bates, Kenneth A. Dodge, David M. Ferguson, L. John Horwood, Gregory S. Pettit, and Lianne Woodward. " Does Father Absence Place Daughters at Special Risk for Early Sexual Activity and Teenage Pregnancy." Child Development 74 (May/June 2003): 801-821.

Griffin, Kenneth W., Gilbert J.Botvin, Lawrence M.Scheier, Tracy Diaz and Nicole L. Miller. "Parenting Practices as Predictors of Substance use, Delinquency, and Aggression Among Urban Minority Youth: Moderating Effects of Family Structure and Gender." Psychology of Addictive Behaviors 14 (June 2000): 174-184.

Matthews, T.J., Sall C.Curtin, and Marian F. MacDorman. Infant Mortality Statistics from the 19989 Period Linked Birth/Infant Death Data Set. National Vital Statistics Reports, Vol 48, No. 12. Hyattsville, MD: National Center for Health Statistics, 2000.

National Center for Education Statistics. The Condition of Education. NCES 1999022. Washington, D.C.: US Dept. of Education, 1999: 76.

Nord, Christine Winquist, and Jerry West. Fathers' and Mothers' Involvement in Their Children's Schools by Family Type and Residential Status. (NCES 2001-032). Washington, D.C.: U.S. Department of Education, National Centre for Education Statistics, 2001.

Sediak, Andrea J. and Diane Broadhurst. The Third National Incidence Study of Child Abuse and Neglect: Final Report.

U.S. Department of Health and Human Services. National Teachman, Jay D. "The Childhood Living Arrangements of Children and the Characteristics of Their Marriages." Journal of Family Issues 25 (January 2004): 86-111.Center on Child Abuse and Neglect. Washington, D.C., September 1996.

Sorenson, Elaine and Chava Zibman. "Getting to Know Poor Fathers

Who Do Not Pay Child Support." Social Service Review 75 (September 2001): 420-434.

U.S. Census Bureau, Children's Living Arrangements and Characteristics: March 2002, P200-547, Table C8. Washington D.C.:GPO, 2003.

U.S. Department of Health and Human Services. National Centre for Health Statistics. Survey on Child Health. Washington, D.C.: GPO, 1993.

BOOKS

Campbell, Ross. M. 1983. *HOW TO REALLY LOVE YOUR TEENAGER.*
Heaton, Illinois: SP Publications Inc.

Campbell, Ross. M. 1987. *HOW TO REALLY LOVE YOUR CHILD.*
Heaton, Illinois: SP Publications Inc.

Dobson, James. 1976. *DARE TO DISCIPLINE.* Wheaton, Illinois: Tyndale House Publishers.

Goldberg, Louis. 1990. *THE PRACTICAL WISDOM OF PROVERBS.* Grand Rapids: Kregel Publications.

Macdonald, Gordon. 1989. *DIE EFFEKTIEWE VADER.* Wheaton,
Illinois: Tyndale House Publishers.

McGlason, E. T. 2013. *THE FATHER YOU'VE ALWAYS WANTED.* USA: Baker Book House Company.

Meier, Paul. D. 1977. *CHRISTIAN CHILD REARING AND PERSONALITY DEVELOPMENT.* USA: Baker Book House Company.

Prince, Derek. 2000. *HUSBANDS AND FATHERS.* Derek Prince Ministries.

There is an SAQA accredited, well-developed rehabilitation program available at my practise CHAPTER NOVA in 893, Tiptol Street, SILVERTON, PRETORIA. Training and counseling are available in R-E-P-A-I-R- the B-R-O-K-E-N-

R- EPENT
E- NTHUSIASM
P- RIORITIES
A- CCEPTANCE
I- NTROSPECTION
R- ELATIONSHIPS

the

B- ARRIERS
R- EJECTED
O- FFENDED
K- AMIKAZE SYNDROME
E- MOTIONAL
N- EGATIVISM

The Story Behind the Cover of this Book

The Solid Ground on which a family stands are determined by the relationship the Father has with his Child.

No matter how dark everything around us seems to be, when you keep your focus on God, there will always be a bright light showing you the way.

By building your relationship with God, it puts your feet on Solid Ground while you lead your family and the community towards a better future.

Sonja Pitzer

www.ingramcontent.com/pod-product-compliance
Lightning Source LLC
Chambersburg PA
CBHW031139250726
48655CB00002B/740